# Billy and Me
# and the Igloo
## and other poems

## Eric Finney

## Pictures by Sue Heap

Edward Arnold

© Eric Finney 1986
Illustrations © Sue Heap 1986

First published in Great Britain 1986 by
Edward Arnold (Publishers) Ltd
41 Bedford Square, London WC1B 3DQ

Edward Arnold (Australia) Pty Ltd
80 Waverley Road, Caulfield East
Victoria 3145, Australia

**British Cataloguing in Publication Data**

Finney, Eric
  Billy and me and the igloo.—(Billy and me)
  I. Title    II. Heap,Sue
  821 '.914    PR6056.I518/

  ISBN 0–7131–7392–0

**Riddles**
Bra
Onion
Snowman
Question mark

Text set in 12/15pt Century
by The Castlefield Press, Moulton, Northampton
Printed in Great Britain by Butler & Tanner Ltd, Frome, Somerset
and bound by W H Ware and Sons Ltd, Clevedon, Avon

# Contents

# Billy and Me and the Igloo

School again in January after the Christmas holiday:
Nobody very keen;
Next Christmas a million light years away,
And a load of toil in between.
Still, like our Billy says,
"You've got to make the best of it man,"
And I must say the mighty snowfall helped –
It came right in the middle of Jan.

You could tell waking up there was something strange,
Something all muffled and bright,
And Billy yells out from our bedroom window,
"Hey, it snowed like the clappers last night!"
"More to come," says Dad when we get downstairs,
He's been outside shovelling the drive.
"No point in going to school," says Billy.
"It's a perfect day to skive."
"Rubbish!" says Mum and she fills us with porridge
And fry-up and tea till we just can't take any more,
Then she loads us with wellies and socks and sweaters
And coats and gloves and bobble hats and scarves
    galore –
And pushes us through the door.

There were socking great drifts on the way to school
And the plunging and diving were great,
And so was the snowballing,
But when we got there
We were both in a bit of a state –
And late.
Not that it mattered, 'cos things weren't normal –

The place was all quiet and queer;
"I told you," said Billy, "we ought to've skived off,
There's hardly anyone here."
Less than half a school full of kids heard the boss
At assembly in the hall:
"The eye marvels at the beauty of its whiteness
And the mind is amazed at its fall . . ."

And blow me, even as he's rabbiting on
It's coming again in masses,
And with everybody gawping through the window
Instead of listening,
The old boy packs it in
And sends us back to classes.

Our Sir's managed to get to school
Though some of the teachers are away:
I suppose they'll be lying in bed
Watching video nasties all day.

On a day like this with about half a class
It's a question of what to do:
I mean there's not much point in doing decimals (ha, ha)
Or the Battle of Waterloo.
So Sir let us read or chat or play draughts
Or mooch about or whatever,
And some of us stood at the windows
Just gazing out at the weather;
I got in a sort of zombie trance,
A kind of hypnotic state,
Just watching it pelting down snowflakes
At a mad fantastic rate.

At playtime it's on with the wellies and gear
And into the white world we go,
And we're rolling and kicking and diving
And chucking – and all getting plastered with snow.
In wellies, down necks, up jumpers it was
And Sir really decided to hate us
When we came in, and spread snow all over his room
And wet clothes on his radiators.

So for the next half hour it's strictly business
And noses down to the grind,
But I'm reading this great book called 'Stig of the
    Dump',
So I don't really mind.
When we look up it's stopped snowing
And Sir stops sulking soon
And he asks if we've got any bright ideas
About what to do in the afternoon.
"We could build an igloo," said Billy.
"We've got all the materials we need here,
Besides I've been reading how Eskimos do it
In an old encyclopedia."
Sir said he thought a lot of eskies now
Didn't build igloos at all,
But lived in houses with toasters and tellies
And carpets wall to wall,
And instead of blubber lamps he reckoned
They probably had microwaves to cook,
But Billy said he preferred to think
About the Eskimo in his old book:
The picture of him in the Polar wastes
Was really very nice –
All snuggled up in furs and dangling his line
In a little hole in the ice.

Anyway, that was the idea he'd got of eskies
And he was blooming sticking to it;
Then Sir said the igloo was a great idea,
And how would Billy do it?

After dinner we piled all the clothing back on –
Like Eskimos in their fur –
Then we revealed the secret preparations
Made by Billy and me and Sir:
In the P.E. shed we'd found two old boxes,
Quite long and strong and wide,
And we'd knocked the bottoms out of them both
And nailed a handle on each side;
We'd got spades as well, a skipping-rope,
Two cricket stumps and a board,
And the first job went to the terrible twins,
Mabel and Peter Ward;
Billy was foreman and he chose them
As the ones to make a start –
So they tied the rope to the cricket stumps
A yard and a bit apart.
We chose a flat site and Peter planted
His cricket stump in the ground,
Then Mabel, keeping the skipping-rope tight,
Drew a circle by walking around.

Of course Sir gave a lecture, like teachers do,
(As if we really cared)
About the circumference of circles and radii
And something called pie are squared.
Somebody had to do something to stop him
So I faked a bad fit of sneezing,
And Elsie and Eileen began coughing like mad
And Billy said he was freezing.
"Better get cracking then," said Sir,
"A squad of you to each box."
And we all started cramming the snow in tight
To make the building blocks.

I bet you thought that an igloo was made
By piling loose snow for the wall,
But according to Billy's encyclopedia
It's not done like that at all.
Billy said Eskimos slice the blocks
With their knives from drifts of snow,
But that might be slightly advanced for us
So we gave the box method a go.

It worked a treat: get it ram jam full
Then scrape the top surface flat,
A bit of a jerk and lift by the handles –
There's your snow block lying pat.
We carried the blocks to the igloo site
Very gingerly on the board –
Sir wanted to talk about cuboids and things
But was totally ignored.
We soon had the base layer of blocks set out
Round the circle neat as a pin,
Then we're putting a second layer up
On the first, but a bit set in.

The blockmakers and blocklayers now
Are really bending their backs
And the rest of the team are filling and smoothing
The ledges and steps and cracks.
It's a thriller watching that igloo grow
From just snow to a kind of a home,
Every layer taking it in a bit
And closer to closing the dome.
Sir's been working like one of the kids
But he's looking distinctly blue,
So we let him pop off for a bit of a warm
And a cup of the staffroom brew.

By the time he's back, the top is closed
Except for a hole for air,
And we're scraping and smoothing away at the sides
And burrowing a way in there.
Billy and me are the first through the hole –
It's a pretty ragged scene,
But ten minutes trimming and scraping away
And it's fit for the duke and the queen.
The rest have been building the entrance tunnel
And they've really been doing their stuff:
Fats went down on all fours,
And they built it round him
To be sure it was big enough.

And it's suddenly done, and everyone
Stands back to take a look,
And Billy says it looks quite like
The one in his musty old book.
By now we're all starting to feel pretty cold
In wet gloves and wet socks and wet jeans;
Sir wonders how many could squeeze inside
And eight of us do like sardines.
A lot of the kids from the rest of the school
Trooped out to take look-sees,
And so did the boss, and would you believe,
He crawls in on his hands and knees!

Next day Charlie Jones from the local rag
Took some photos that turned out top-hole:
There was one like that picture of Captain Scott
And his men at the South Pole.
It's got all the builders on, including Sir
And Mabel and Peter and Fats,
And Billy and me, well you can't miss us –
Side by side in the bobble hats.

There's more than four hundred kids at our school
And during the next week or two,
There couldn't be many who didn't come out
And get into our famous igloo.
Of course, before they crawled inside
They asked for our permission –
"We could've made a fortune," Billy said,
"By charging for admission."

And that igloo lasted for ages and ages –
You could see it from our class:
A crumbling ruin, a bit smaller each day,
Grubby white on the springtime grass.

# Summer Term Outing

Sing hey nonny nonny, the open road,
Beloved of Ratty and Moley and Toad,
Now we're on our way with the sick-bags stowed –
 We're off on our summer term outing.

We'd eaten our lunches by nine fifteen,
And soon after that we saw little Eileen
Was turning a very peculiar green –
 On the bus, on our summer term outing.

First stop was a castle; we went up the keep,
And Miss down below just collapsed in a heap
When she saw Neville Stephens pretending to leap
 From the top, on our summer term outing.

opening
hours

Most of the day was spent drinking and munchin',
Though we didn't feel much like eating our luncheon
After the grottiness down in the dungeon,
   That day, on our summer term outing.

So we lunched in a field, with buttercups petalled,
And most of the class had just got nicely settled
When Karen fell over a cow and got nettled
   On her legs, at our summer term outing.

He's a very good driver that Mr O'Keefe:
We all needed a loo, and were gritting our teeth —
So he stopped at some bushes: cor, what a relief
   For the kids on our summer term outing.

We were on our way home at a quarter past four,
And Miss went to sleep: she didn't half snore!
But we were all lively and ready for more
   At the end of our summer term outing.

# Don't Panic

That beating at my bedroom pane:
It's only wind and driving rain.
Relax.

That awful blind and blurry mass:
Nothing but rain streaks on the glass.
Harmless.

That monstrous shadow leaning in,
Wearing an evil twisted grin:
It's just the ivy plant that's all,
Bobbing and tossing on the wall.
Don't panic.

That scratching from my bedroom floor:
It's just a mouse, he's been before.
No sweat.

That rustling – is it just the draught?
Or giant spiders? Don't be daft!
Couldn't be.

The loops this new wallpaper makes:
Just loops, not coiled and deadly snakes.
                    Absurd!

Suppose there are though – snakes, I mean,
And evil spirits sidling in,
And ghosts and blobs and phantom riders
And armies of advancing spiders,
And vampires stalking through the gloom,
All closing in upon my room . . .

17

# Snail

No knowing
Where you're going,
Slow tracker,
Backpacker;
You won't get
There just yet.

Easily seen
Where you've been.

# Grub

A grub in an apple
   is a menace and a curse.
But half a grub
   in half an apple's worse.

# Instant Revenge

Better not annoy me –
I've got this terrible power, see;
I don't boast about it a lot
But instant revenge is what I've got.
Somebody, anybody, gets on my wick,
Revenge is dreadful and very quick –
Happens as fast as your eye can blink,
Happens, in fact, as fast as I can think.
Frinstances? Well, here's a few –
I've witnesses to prove they're true:
The Head in assembly called me a fool:
His trousers fell down in front of the school;
A neighbour refused to give back my ball:
Cracks instantly appeared in his new front wall;
The check-out girl ignored me – went on chatting
    to a chap:
Her till disintegrated – fell right in her lap;
The bully snatched my hat off and dumped me in the
    ditch:
He immediately got hiccups and a violent itch;
Our teacher accused me of copying sums:
Her false teeth promptly dropped right off her gums;
Another day she stopped my games on the field:
Her wig came off and her egg was revealed.

Don't ask me how I do it – it defies explanation,
It's all in my power of concentration.
Try it yourself me old fruit, me old flower –
You might find you've got the power.

# The Things They Say

Mum's fitting a new dustbin liner
After the dustman's been.
Says,
"This dustbin's so clean
It'd stand inspection by the queen."
And I get this mental picture . . .
Queen makes official visit to our town
In her coach with her robes
And jewels and crown;
Makes a special diversion to see our bin,
Spends quite some time
Bending over, peering in.
Moment captured by cameraman of 'Daily Deeds' –
Front page picture, caption reads:
"BIN IMMACULATELY CLEAN
SAYS QUEEN."

And Dad's got this joke –
It's getting quite a bore –
About our town football team
Who can't score.
We're swinging happily off to the match
And away again goes Dad:
"I don't know why I keep going
To see the Rovers –
They never come to see me
When I'm bad."
But they might one day . . .
Dad's in bed with flu, half-dead, half-alive,
Saturday afternoon,
About a quarter to five;
Exuberant ring at the front doorbell,
Answered by Mum; enter pell-mell
The Rovers, all of them, in muddy shirts and boots
Complete with manager
And two substitutes.

Troop noisily upstairs to where Dad's lying.
"How do, old lad, we heard you were dying.
Came to cheer you up, delighted to say
We only lost seventeen-nil today."

And then there's my Gran:
Maybe you're picking your nose a bit
Or peeling back a scab,
And my Gran's sure to say,
As she gives your hand a dab,
"Don't do that, my darling, or
It'll turn into a pig's foot."
And suppose it does . . . my nose, I mean,
Begin to grow and shoot –
And instead of a nose there's a trotter
All pink and bristly and grotty . . .
Why does she say such things?
Honest, she's potty!

But the worst picture I get
Is when our teacher produces
The Ultimate Threat:
"Do that again," he says,
"I'll have your guts for garters,"
And my mind's eye sees a red mess –
Like a load of squashed tomatoes –
With lots of rubbery, twangy bits
And tubes and pipes and strings,
And Sir with scissors
Cutting garter-sized rings . . .

Better not go on – don't want you sick today;
I just wish they'd watch some of
The Things They Say.

# Wet Playtime

The window's blurred with rain,
Outside it pelts and pours,
The playground's one big pimpled puddle;
Sir goes for morning tea,
Says, "Settle down indoors,
Behave yourselves; don't make a muddle."

. . . .

So what do we do to keep off the gloom
On a rotten wet day shut up in our room?
Well, Neville has always been curious to know:
Can he scratch his left ear with his right foot big toe?
So he's trying it now, while Jonathan Rose
Is making his pen disappear up his nose;

The Robinson twins (nicknamed Bigears and Noddy)
Are giggling over a book called "Your Body,"
And Eileen's got chalk and is drawing – good lord! –
A horrible picture of Sir on the board.
There's a buzz from some kids who are racing the snails:
Flash leading but Fred's coming up on the rails;

25

There's battleship bombing across at the sink –
The water's about to slop over, I think –
Ooh yes, now it has and it's all pouring through
To the cupboard where Sir keeps spare rolls for the loo;
And now, would you believe it, some great clumsy ox
Has spilt powder-paint in the dressing-up box!
And the rest of the class? Well, I won't spell it out,
But the rest of the class are just mucking about . . .

"Sir's coming!"
We all rush at no end of a rate
To hide all things wet, bent or bust,
And we're all reading nicely,
And Sir says, "That's great,
I see you're a class I can trust."

# Our Solar System

We made a model of the Solar System today
On our school field after lunch.
Sir chose nine of us
To be planets
And he parked the rest of the class
In the middle of the field
In a thoroughly messy bunch.
"You're the sun," he brays,
"Big, huge; stick your arms out
In all directions
To show the sun's rays."
The bit about sticking arms out
Really wasn't very wise
And I don't mind telling you
A few fingers and elbows
Got stuck in a few eyes.

Big Bill took a poke at Tony
And only narrowly missed him,
And altogether it looked
More like a shambles
Than the start of the Solar System.
The nine of us who were planets
Didn't get a lot of fun:
I was Mercury and I stood
Like a Charlie
Nearest of all to the sun,
And all the sun crowd
Blew raspberries and shouted,

"This is the one we'll roast!
We're going to scorch you up, Titch,
You'll be like a black slice of toast!"
Katy was Venus and Val was Earth
And Neville Stephens was Mars,
And the sun kids shouted and
Wanted to know
Could he spare them any of his Bars.

A big gap then to Jupiter (Jayne)
And a bigger one still to Saturn,
And Sir's excited and rambling on
About the System's mighty pattern.
"Now, a walloping space to Uranus," he bawls,
"It's quite a bike ride away from the sun."
Ha blooming ha – at least somebody here's
Having a load of fun.
He's got two planet kids left
And Karen's moaning
About having to walk so far:

She's Neptune – I suppose Sir's
Cracking some joke about
Doing x million miles by car.
Pete's Pluto – "The farthest flung of all,"
Says Sir,
He's put by the hedge and rests,
But soon he starts picking blackberries
And poking at old birds' nests.
"Of course," yells Sir, "the scale's not right
But it'll give you
A rough idea.
Now, when I blow my whistle
I want you all to start on your orbits –
Clear?"
Well, it wasn't of course,
And most of the class, well,
Their hearts weren't really in it,
Still, Sir's O.K. so we gave it a go,
With me popping round the sun
About ten times a minute,
And Pluto on the hedge ambling round
Fit to finish his orbit next year.
We'd still have been there but
A kid came out of school and yelled,
"The bell's gone and the school bus's here!"
Well, the Solar System
Broke up pretty fast,
And my bus money had gone from my sock
And I had to borrow.
I suppose we'll have to draw diagrams
And write about it tomorrow.

# Navels 15p

That's just what the sign
On the shop said:
NAVELS 15p.
"Well," I thought, "at that price
I might buy two or three."
I'd always fancied a replacement
For my lumpy old blob –
I mean, every other kid
Seemed to have
A real neat job.
But belly-buttons in that shop?
Mostly veg and fruit on show . . .
Navels just a sideline perhaps –
Anyway, in we go.
"Yes sir, what can we sell you?
Some lovely melons this week;
Purple sprouting broccoli?
Grapes are at their peak."
"You're advertising navels,
They don't seem awfully dear.
Could you show me what's available;
It's got to fit in here."
And I hitched my tee-shirt
Up a bit
To show this bloke the spot.
He looked at me rather oddly,
Said, "I'll show you what I've got."
He took an orange from the rack
And showed me the end of the fruit.
"Pity it's on an orange," I said.
"That one would just suit."

# Four Riddles

Twin-tubbed
Warm-hearted thing;
A sling.

Pinky brown, then farther in
Green, then white and skin on skin.
So to the knife, the pot is calling –
It's not for sadness tears are falling.

Poor, pale fellow:
You'll run
In the sun.

It's after the asking,
It's nearly a noose,
It's a crook,
It's a hook
With a blob that's come loose.